INTEGRATING
Our Country and World
with Reading Instruction

6 Complete Social Studies Units

Written by
Trisha Callella

Editor: LaDawn Walter
Illustrator: Jenny Campbell
Cover Illustrator: Rick Grayson
Designer/Production: Moonhee Pak/Mary Gagné
Cover Designer: Moonhee Pak
Art Director: Tom Cochrane
Project Director: Carolea Williams

Table of Contents

Introduction   3

Connections to Standards   4

Unit Overview   5

American Symbols
Prereading Strategies 9

Nonfiction Text 12

Postreading Applications 14

Hands-on Social Studies 17

National Holidays
Prereading Strategies 21

Nonfiction Text 24

Postreading Applications 26

Hands-on Social Studies 29

Making a Law
Prereading Strategies 32

Nonfiction Text 35

Postreading Applications 37

Hands-on Social Studies 40

Continents
Prereading Strategies 42

Nonfiction Text 45

Postreading Applications 47

Hands-on Social Studies 50

Bodies of Water
Prereading Strategies 53

Nonfiction Text 56

Postreading Applications 58

Hands-on Social Studies 61

Ancestors
Prereading Strategies 63

Nonfiction Text 66

Postreading Applications 68

Hands-on Social Studies 71

Introduction

For many children, reading comprehension diminishes when they read nonfiction text. Children often have difficulty understanding social studies vocabulary, making inferences, and grasping social studies concepts. With so much curriculum to cover each day, social studies content is sometimes put on the back burner when it comes to academic priorities. *Integrating Our Country and World with Reading Instruction* provides the perfect integration of social studies content with specific reading instruction to help children improve their comprehension of nonfiction text and maximize every minute of your teaching day.

This resource includes six units that relate to our country and world. The units are based on the most common social studies topics taught in grades 1–2 in accordance with the national social studies standards:

American Symbols   **Continents**
National Holidays   **Bodies of Water**
Making a Law   **Ancestors**

Each unit includes powerful prereading strategies, such as predicting what the story will be about, accessing prior knowledge, and brainstorming about vocabulary that may be included in the reading selection. Following the prereading exercises is a nonfiction reading selection written on a grade 1–2 reading level. Each reading selection is followed by essential postreading activities such as comprehension questions on multiple taxonomy levels, skill reviews, and a critical thinking exercise. Each unit also includes a hands-on experience that connects each social studies topic to children's lives. The descriptions on pages 5–8 include the objectives and implementation strategies for each unit component.

Before, during, and after reading the story, children are exposed to the same reading strategies you typically reinforce during your language arts instruction block and guided reading. This powerful duo gives you the opportunity to teach both reading and social studies simultaneously. Using the activities in this resource, children will continue *learning to read* while *reading to learn*. They will become more successful readers while gaining new social studies knowledge and experiences.

Prereading Strategies

✓ Catch a Clue
✓ Concept Map
✓ Word Warm-Up

Nonfiction Text

Postreading Applications

✓ Comprehension Questions
✓ Sharpen Your Skills
✓ Get Logical

Hands-on Social Studies

Connections to Standards

This chart shows the concepts that are covered in each unit based on the national social studies standards.

	American Symbols	National Holidays	Making a Law	Continents	Bodies of Water	Ancestors
Gain an understanding of cultural unity and diversity within and across groups.	●	●				●
Compare and contrast differences about past events, people, places, or situations.	●	●				●
Understand how experiences may be interpreted differently by people from diverse cultural perspectives and frames of reference.						●
Learn about the unique features of one's nuclear and extended families.						●
Understand the significance of national holidays and the people associated with them.	●	●				
Identify American symbols, landmarks, and essential documents.	●	●				
Examine the purpose of rules and laws.			●			
Understand the tensions between the wants and needs of individuals and groups.			●			
Examine rights and responsibilities.			●			
Locate and distinguish landforms and geographic features such as mountains, islands, and oceans.				●	●	
Compare a three-dimensional model to a picture of the same location.				●	●	
Locate on maps and globes the seven continents and four oceans.				●	●	

Unit Overview

Catch a Clue

Objectives

Children will

✓ be introduced to key concepts and vocabulary *before* reading

✓ be able to transfer this key strategy to improve test-taking skills

Implementation

Children will use clues and the process of elimination to predict what the nonfiction reading selection will be about. Copy this page on an overhead transparency, and use it for a whole-class activity. Begin by reading aloud each word, and ask children to repeat the words. Read the clues one at a time. Then, discuss with the class what topic(s) could be eliminated and the reasons why. (Note: There will be clues that do not eliminate any topics. The purpose of this is to teach children that although there is information listed, it is not always helpful information.) Cross off a topic when the class decides that it does not fit the clues. If there is more than one topic left after the class discusses all of the clues, this becomes a prediction activity. When this occurs, reread the clues with the class, and discuss which answer would be most appropriate given the clues provided.

Concept Map

Objectives

Children will

✓ access prior knowledge by brainstorming what they already know about the topic

✓ increase familiarity with the social studies content by hearing others' prior knowledge experiences

✓ revisit the map *after* reading to recall information from the reading selection

Implementation

Copy this page on an overhead transparency, and use it for a whole-class activity. Use a colored pen to write children's prior knowledge on the transparency. After the class reads the story, use a different colored pen to add what children learned.

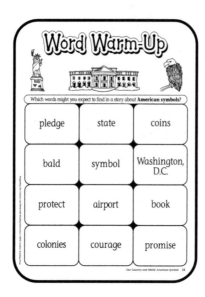

Word Warm-Up

Objectives

Children will

✓ be introduced to new vocabulary words

✓ make predictions about the story using thinking and reasoning skills

✓ begin to monitor their own comprehension

Implementation

Children will use the strategy of exclusion brainstorming to identify which words are likely to be in the story and which words are unrelated and should be eliminated from the list. Copy this page on an overhead transparency, and use it for a whole-class activity. Have children make predictions about which of the vocabulary words could be in the story and which words probably would not be in the story. Ask them to give reasons for their predictions. For example, say *Do you think rules would be in a story about laws?* A child may say *Yes, because rules are the same as laws* or *No, because rules are only for school.* Circle the word if a child says that it will be in the story, and cross it out if a child says it will not be in the story. Do not correct children's responses. After reading, children can either confirm or disconfirm their own predictions. It is more powerful for children to verify their predictions on their own than to be told the answer before ever reading the story.

Nonfiction Text

The Story

Objectives

Children will

✓ read high-interest, nonfiction stories

✓ increase social studies knowledge

✓ increase content area vocabulary

✓ make connections between the social studies facts and their own experiences

Implementation

Give each child a copy of the story, and display the corresponding Word Warm-Up transparency while you read the story with the class. After the class reads the story, go back to the transparency, and have children discuss their predictions in relation to the new information they learned in the story. Invite children to identify any changes they would make on the transparency and give reasons for their responses. Then, revisit the corresponding Concept Map transparency, and write the new information children have learned.

Postreading Applications

Comprehension Questions

Objectives

Children will

✓ recall factual information

✓ be challenged to think beyond the story facts to make inferences

✓ connect the story to other reading, their own lives, and the world around them

Implementation

Use these questions to facilitate a class discussion of the story. Choose the number and types of questions that best meet the abilities of your class.

Sharpen Your Skills

Objectives

Children will

✓ practice answering questions in common test-taking formats

✓ integrate language arts skills with social studies knowledge

Implementation

After the class reads a story, give each child a copy of this page. Ask children to read each question and all of the answer choices for that question before deciding on an answer. Show them how to use their pencil to completely fill in the circle for their answer. Invite children to raise their hand if they have difficulty reading a question and/or the answer choices. Thoroughly explain the types of questions and exactly what is being asked the first few times children use this reproducible.

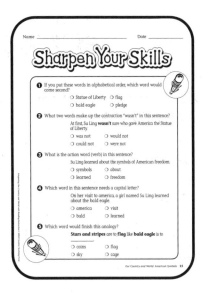

Get Logical

Objectives

Children will

✓ practice logical and strategic thinking skills

✓ practice the skill of process of elimination

✓ transfer the information read by applying it to new situations

Implementation

Give each child a copy of this page. Read the beginning sentences and the clues to familiarize children with the words. Show children step-by-step how to eliminate choices based on the clues given. Have children place an X in a box that represents an impossible choice, thereby narrowing down the options for accurate choices. Once children understand the concept, they can work independently on this reproducible.

Hands-on Social Studies

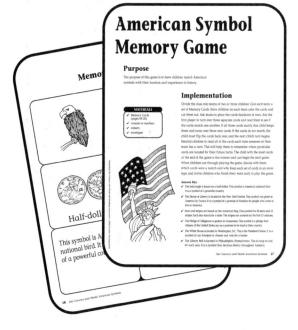

Social Studies Activity

Objectives

Children will

✓ participate in hands-on learning experiences

✓ expand and reinforce social studies knowledge

✓ apply new social studies vocabulary words

Implementation

The social studies activities in this book incorporate a variety of skills children are required to experience at this age level (e.g., survey, interview, analyze, evaluate). Each hands-on activity begins with an explanation of its purpose to help direct the intended learning. Give each child a copy of any corresponding reproducibles and/or materials for the activity. Then, introduce the activity and explain the directions. Model any directions that may be difficult for children to follow on their own.

Catch a Clue

Integrating Our Country and World with Reading Instruction © 2002 Creative Teaching Press

What will we learn about in our reading today?

American presidents

American symbols

African countries

flags around the world

Our Clues

❶ We will focus on the continent of North America.

❷ The focus will be on people's freedoms.

❸ We will learn about the bald eagle and a flag.

Concept Map

Facts we already know about **American symbols,** and the new facts we have learned

American Symbols

Integrating Our Country and World with Reading Instruction © 2002 Creative Teaching Press

Word Warm-Up

Which words might you expect to find in a story about **American symbols?**

pledge	state	coins
bald	symbol	Washington, D.C.
protect	airport	book
colonies	courage	promise

American Symbols

"Let's go Luke! We do not want to be late to pick up Su Ling. She is coming to America for the first time," said my mom. We got in the car and drove to the airport. Our new friend walked off the plane. She had wanted to visit for a long time. Now, she was finally here!

Su Ling saw me holding up the American flag. She remembered that the flag was a symbol of America. Her teacher told her that a symbol reminds you of something. She was so happy to be in America! I gave her the flag.

In the car, Su Ling asked why our flag was different than the flag of China. I told her that each star stands for a state. The stripes are symbols for the first thirteen colonies. The flag is a symbol of the freedoms the American people fought for. I also told her how the colors of the flag were chosen for their meaning. The red stands for courage. The white stands for liberty. The blue stands for loyalty. I told her that when Americans display the flag,

Integrating Our Country and World with Reading Instruction © 2002 Creative Teaching Press

it is to keep in mind the people who gave up their lives for freedom. Su Ling said she was going to put the flag next to the Statue of Liberty poster we sent to her last fall.

"I remember when you gave me the poster," Su Ling said. "I asked who the lady was with the crown on her head!" We all laughed. "You told me she was a statue in the New York Harbor. You also said the people of France gave the statue to America. You told me it has been in America since 1885. You said it is a promise of freedom for people who come to live in America."

I also told her about the bald eagle. It is America's national bird. It is a big and strong bird. It lives a long time. It was chosen as a symbol of a powerful country. I showed her a silver dollar and some quarters. I showed her the bald eagle on each one. Then, I gave her the coins to add to her collection of American symbols. "I cannot send you home with a real bald eagle, so this will just have to do," I said.

Comprehension Questions

Integrating Our Country and World with Reading Instruction © 2002 Creative Teaching Press

Literal Questions

1. Name three symbols of American freedom.

2. Where can you find the bald eagle as a symbol?

3. How many stars and stripes are on the American flag? What do they represent?

4. Where did the Statue of Liberty come from?

Inferential Questions

1. Why do you think America has symbols for its country?

2. Do you think that other countries have the same symbols as America? Why or why not?

3. If America did not have the symbols you read about in the story, how would Americans' lives be different?

4. How old is the Statue of Liberty?

Making Connections

1. Look around your classroom. What symbols do you see? What do they represent?

2. Which American symbol is your favorite? Explain your answer.

3. Make up a new symbol for America. What does it look like? Why did you choose it? What should it remind people of?

Name _____   Date _____

Sharpen Your Skills

1 If you put these words in alphabetical order, which word would come second?

◯ Statue of Liberty   ◯ flag

◯ bald eagle   ◯ pledge

2 What two words make up the contraction "wasn't" in this sentence?

At first, Su Ling **wasn't** sure who gave America the Statue of Liberty.

◯ was not   ◯ would not

◯ could not   ◯ were not

3 What is the action word (verb) in this sentence?

Su Ling learned about the symbols of American freedom.

◯ symbols   ◯ about

◯ learned   ◯ freedom

4 Which word in this sentence needs a capital letter?

On her visit to america, a girl named Su Ling learned about the bald eagle.

◯ america   ◯ visit

◯ bald   ◯ learned

5 Which word would finish this analogy?

Stars and stripes are to **flag** like **bald eagle** is to _____.

◯ coins   ◯ flag

◯ sky   ◯ cage

Integrating Our Country and World with Reading Instruction © 2002 Creative Teaching Press

Name _____   Date _____

Get Logical

Su Ling packed some souvenirs of her trip to America. She packed each souvenir in a different colored suitcase. Use the clues below to decide which suitcase she put each American symbol in.

Clues

❶ She put the American flag in the suitcase that is the same color as one of the colors on the flag.

❷ The souvenir that has pictures of a woman holding a torch was not packed in the green suitcase.

❸ The souvenir of the bald eagle is in her green suitcase.

Statue of Liberty Book			
American Flag			
Quarters			
	Black	Red	Green

The black suitcase has the _____.

The red suitcase has the _____.

The green suitcase has the _____.

Integrating Our Country and World with Reading Instruction © 2002 Creative Teaching Press

American Symbol Memory Game

Purpose

The purpose of this game is to have children match American symbols with their location and importance in history.

Integrating Our Country and World with Reading Instruction © 2002 Creative Teaching Press

MATERIALS

✔ Memory Cards (pages 18–20)
✔ crayons or markers
✔ scissors
✔ envelopes

Implementation

Divide the class into teams of two or three children. Give each team a set of Memory Cards. Have children on each team color the cards and cut them out. Ask teams to place the cards facedown in rows. Ask the first player to turn over three separate cards and read them to see if the cards match one another. If all three cards match, that child keeps them and turns over three new cards. If the cards do not match, the child must flip the cards back over, and the next child's turn begins. Remind children to read all of the cards each time someone on their team has a turn. This will help them to remember where particular cards are located for their future turns. The child with the most cards at the end of the game is the winner and can begin the next game. When children are through playing the game, discuss with them which cards were a match and why. Keep each set of cards in an envelope, and invite children who finish their work early to play the game.

Answer Key

✔ The bald eagle is found on a half-dollar. This symbol is America's national bird. It is a symbol of a powerful country.

✔ The Statue of Liberty is located in the New York Harbor. This symbol was given to America by France. It is a symbol of a promise of freedom for people who come to live in America.

✔ Stars and stripes are found on the American flag. This symbol has 50 stars and 13 stripes. Each star stands for a state. The stripes are symbols for the first 13 colonies.

✔ The Pledge of Allegiance is spoken in classrooms. This symbol is a pledge that citizens of the United States say as a promise to be loyal to their country.

✔ The White House is located in Washington, D.C. This is the President's home. It is a symbol of our freedom to choose and vote for a leader.

✔ The Liberty Bell is located in Philadelphia, Pennsylvania. This is rung on July 4th each year. It is a symbol that declares liberty throughout America.

Memory Cards

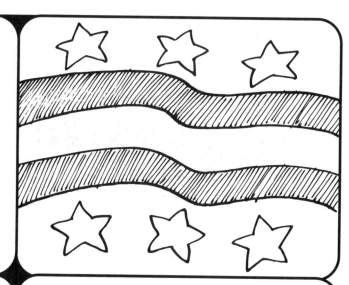

Half-dollar

American Flag

This symbol is America's national bird. It is a symbol of a powerful country.

This symbol has 50 stars and 13 stripes. Each star stands for a state. The stripes are symbols for the first 13 colonies.

Integrating Our Country and World with Reading Instruction © 2002 Creative Teaching Press

Memory Cards

Washington, D.C.

New York Harbor

This is the President's home. It is a symbol of our freedom to choose and vote for a leader.

This symbol was given to America by France. It is a symbol of a promise of freedom for people who come to live in America.

Memory Cards

I pledge allegiance
to the flag
of the United States
of America
and to the Republic
for which it stands,
one Nation under God,
indivisible, with liberty
and justice for all.

Spoken in classrooms

Liberty Bell Pavilion

Philadelphia,
Pennsylvania

This symbol is a pledge that citizens of the United States say as a promise to be loyal to their country.

This is rung on July 4th each year. It is a symbol that declares liberty throughout America.

Integrating Our Country and World with Reading Instruction © 2002 Creative Teaching Press

Catch a Clue

Integrating Our Country and World with Reading Instruction © 2002 Creative Teaching Press

What will we learn about in our reading today?

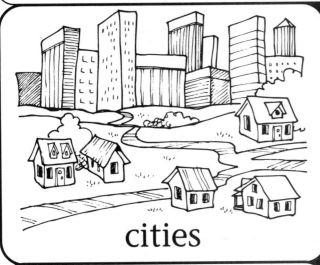

cities

national holidays

flags

presidents

Our Clues

❶ We will learn about people.

❷ They do not change.

❸ They help remind us of the good things people did.

Concept Map

Facts we already know about **national holidays,** and the new facts we have learned

Integrating Our Country and World with Reading Instruction © 2002 Creative Teaching Press

Word Warm-Up

| Which words might you expect to find in a story about **national holidays?** |

president	free	turtles
vote	bullfights	celebrate
stripes	veteran	nation
independence	events	cold

National Holidays

Who celebrates your birthday with you? You might have a party with your family or maybe with your friends. Do you know what would happen if your birthday were a national holiday? All of the people in your nation would celebrate it with you!

Each country has its own holidays. Some are the same. Some are different. A national holiday is a day for people to show pride in their country. It is a day to think about people who lived and things that took place a long time ago. The day may mean a person did something special for a country. It can stand for a big event that helped a nation.

Most nations have a holiday each year on the date they became free. On July 4, 1776, the United States of America became a free country. This day is celebrated each year. It is called Independence Day. Canada has the same holiday on July 1st. People light fireworks, have picnics, and play music on this day. Mexico

Integrating Our Country and World with Reading Instruction © 2002 Creative Teaching Press

celebrates on September 16th. They have rodeos, parades, bullfights, and lots of food!

The United States has other national holidays, too. One of them is Veterans Day. Many people have fought to keep our country free. Some people were hurt. Some people died. This is the day to think about these people. It is good to give thanks for their help.

The United States has a holiday called Presidents' Day. It was started to give thanks for a good president. His name was George Washington. Do you know which president he was? Another very good president was Abraham Lincoln. They both did a lot to help the country. Their birthdays were in the same month. We celebrate their birthdays and all of the good ways they helped the country on Presidents' Day.

The next time there is a national holiday, remember to think about the people and events that helped the country.

Comprehension Questions

Literal Questions

1 What is a national holiday?

2 What is Independence Day?

3 What is Veterans Day?

4 What is Presidents' Day?

Inferential Questions

1 Why do you think different countries have different national holidays?

2 Why do you think different countries celebrate a similar holiday in different ways?

3 Why do you think it is important to remember certain days, people, and events?

4 Do you think Presidents' Day now also represents other presidents as well? Why?

Making Connections

1 Which is your favorite national holiday? Why? What do you do to celebrate it?

2 Are there any national holidays in the same month as your birthday? Which ones?

3 In the story, you read about how different countries celebrate holidays. Which sounded the most fun to you? Why?

Integrating Our Country and World with Reading Instruction © 2002 Creative Teaching Press

Sharpen Your Skills

1 If you put these words in alphabetical order, which word would come first?

- ○ president   ○ holiday
- ○ celebrate   ○ birthday

2 What two words make up the contraction "don't" in this sentence?

People around the world **don't** always celebrate the same national holidays.

- ○ did not   ○ will not
- ○ does not   ○ do not

3 Which word in this sentence needs a capital letter?

A national holiday people celebrate in the United States is veterans Day.

- ○ veterans   ○ holiday
- ○ people   ○ celebrate

4 Which word best completes this sentence?

A national holiday reminds us of the people and events that were important in _____ our country.

- ○ help   ○ helping
- ○ helped   ○ helpers

5 Which word would finish this analogy?

July 4th is to the **U.S.A.** like **September 16th** is to _____.

- ○ Canada   ○ America
- ○ Mexico   ○ Australia

Get Logical

Brett, Chloe, and Dane each have a favorite national holiday. Use the clues below to decide which national holiday each person likes to celebrate the most.

Clues

1 Chloe lives in Canada. She likes picnics and fireworks.

2 Brett lives in America. His birthday is in February. He wants to be like George Washington when he grows up.

3 Dane's grandpa was in World War II. He is proud that his grandpa helped protect the United States.

	Brett	Chloe	Dane
Presidents' Day			
Independence Day			
Veterans Day			

Brett likes _____ the best.

Chloe likes _____ the best.

Dane likes _____ the best.

National Holiday Banners

Purpose

The purpose of this activity is for children to learn the history behind various national holidays and gain an understanding as to why they do not have school on those days.

MATERIALS

✔ National Holiday Research reproducible (page 30)

✔ National Holiday Banner reproducible (page 31)

✔ books on national holidays

✔ magazines

✔ art supplies (e.g., crayons or markers, stickers, glitter)

Implementation

Use this activity for each national holiday your class celebrates (e.g., Memorial Day, Independence Day, Labor Day, Presidents' Day, Veterans Day, Martin Luther King, Jr. Day). Read aloud a book that represents the holiday you are celebrating. Discuss and brainstorm with the class why this holiday is celebrated, symbols used to represent it, and related traditions. List the ideas on the chalkboard. Then, give each child a National Holiday Research reproducible. Ask children to use the information from the board to complete their paper. Give each child a National Holiday Banner reproducible. Ask children to write the name of the holiday in the center of the banner. Invite them to decorate it with symbols that represent the holiday (e.g., pictures from magazines, words and symbols, hand-drawn pictures). Display the completed banners in the classroom.

Name _____   Date _____

National Holiday Research

National holiday: _____

Date celebrated: _____

Why it is celebrated: _____

Important people or place: _____

Two new things I learned about this holiday: _____

_____

_____

National holiday: _____

Date celebrated: _____

Why it is celebrated: _____

Important people or place: _____

Two new things I learned about this holiday: _____

_____

_____

Integrating Our Country and World with Reading Instruction © 2002 Creative Teaching Press

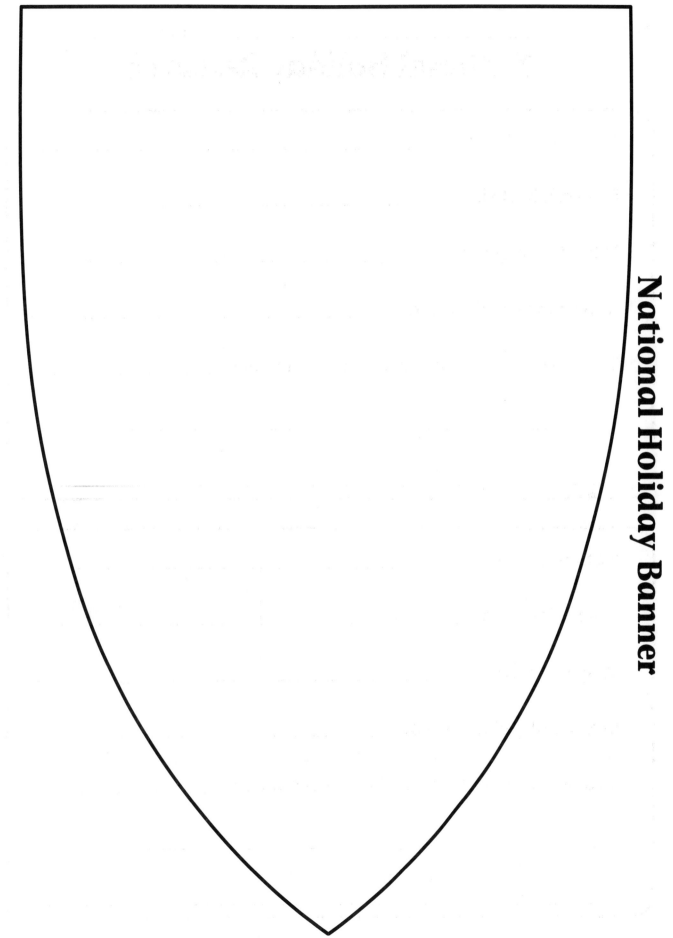

National Holiday Banner

Catch a Clue

laws

dollars

good citizens

police officers

Our Clues

❶ They help keep you safe and protected.

❷ Rules will be part of what we learn about.

❸ People vote and agree on them.

Integrating Our Country and World with Reading Instruction © 2002 Creative Teaching Press

Concept Map

Facts we already know about **laws,** and the new facts we have learned

Laws

Word Warm-Up

Which words might you expect to find in a story about **laws?**

veto	rules	vote
protect	punishment	helmets
compromise	accidents	ticket
seat belt	teacher	pass

Integrating Our Country and World with Reading Instruction © 2002 Creative Teaching Press

Making a Law

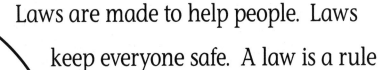

Laws are made to help people. Laws keep everyone safe. A law is a rule that all people must follow if they live in a certain area.

Do you make rules when you play games with your friends? In a way, you are making up the laws of the game. First, you tell everyone what your idea or rule is. Then, you tell them why you think it is a good idea. You also tell them how the rule will help them. To be fair, your friends get to vote on your idea. If most of them agree that your idea will be helpful, then it becomes a rule, or "law." It is the same in your city, state, and country.

Many people were getting hurt in car accidents. Some people thought everyone should wear a seat belt to be safe when riding in a car. This idea was voted on in some states to see if it could become a law. Most people agreed that it was a good idea. This idea became a law. The people also agreed that anyone who chose not to

Integrating Our Country and World with Reading Instruction © 2002 Creative Teaching Press

follow the law would be punished. A ticket is a punishment for drivers who do not follow the safety rules of the road.

Do you like to play in the park? It is nice to live and play in clean areas. Some people saw others throw their trash on the ground. They did not like that. They thought if everyone threw their trash in a trash can, it would help to keep the earth clean. The people voted on this idea. Most people agreed, so it became a law. Now, in many cities, there is a trash law. If you litter, then you will have to pay a fine.

In some states, many children play on skateboards and scooters. A lot of the children were getting hurt. People made a rule that said children should wear helmets when they ride bikes or scooters. The rule was made to help keep children safe. People in some areas agreed that this was a good rule. They voted to make the rule into a law. Now, all children in those areas must wear helmets when they ride on bikes and scooters. Do you wear a helmet when you ride your bike or scooter? Is it a law in your city? What other laws do your city and state have?

Integrating Our Country and World with Reading Instruction © 2002 Creative Teaching Press

Comprehension Questions

Integrating Our Country and World with Reading Instruction © 2002 Creative Teaching Press

? ## Literal Questions

1 What is a law?

2 How are laws made?

3 What rule needs to be followed in some states because of the helmet law?

4 What is an example of a punishment for breaking a law?

 ## Inferential Questions

1 Why are laws important?

2 What would the world around you be like if there were not any laws? Explain your answer.

3 Name two laws in your town. What are the punishments for breaking those laws?

4 Do you think it is a good idea for different states to allow different laws? Why or why not?

 ## Making Connections

1 What laws do you and your family follow? Why do you and your family choose to follow them?

2 What rules, or laws, do you have to follow in your classroom? Are they fair? Why or why not?

3 What rules, or laws, would you like to change at home? Why?

Name _____   Date _____

Sharpen Your Skills

1 If you put these words in alphabetical order, which word would come last?

◯ ideas   ◯ laws

◯ vote   ◯ agree

2 What two words make up the contraction "doesn't" in this sentence?

If you don't like a law, that **doesn't** mean you don't have to follow it.

◯ do not   ◯ did not

◯ does not ◯ didn't not

3 Which word is <u>not</u> a descriptive word (adjective) in this sentence?

Every free land has fair laws that must be obeyed by good citizens.

◯ free   ◯ fair

◯ good   ◯ obeyed

4 Which word best completes this sentence?

The government lets the citizens of the community _____ on what ideas become laws.

◯ voted   ◯ voot

◯ votes   ◯ vote

5 Which word would finish this analogy?

Seat belt is to **safe** like **no helmet** is to _____.

◯ healthy   ◯ smart

◯ game   ◯ unsafe

Integrating Our Country and World with Reading Instruction © 2002 Creative Teaching Press

Get Logical

The Cheyenne City Council is voting on three ideas that may become laws. Three different citizens wrote the three ideas. The three citizens are Benny, Ricardo, and Destry. Use the clues below to decide which idea was created by each citizen.

Clues

❶ Ricardo is tired of listening to his daughter beg for a new pair of pants. They cost too much money for him to buy.

❷ Benny is going to college. He studies at night after work. It is too noisy for him to study.

❸ Destry wants to help the earth.

	Benny	Ricardo	Destry
No loud noises after 10:00 p.m.			
Children must wear uniforms.			
Each family must recycle cans and plastic.			

Benny's idea is _____.

Ricardo's idea is _____.

Destry's idea is _____.

Making New Laws

Purpose

The purpose of this activity is to empower children in the area of government and to give them an opportunity to experience the democratic process of making a law. "Every vote counts" is hard for children to comprehend. This activity will help show them that they really can make a difference.

MATERIALS

✔ Drafting a New Law reproducible (page 41)

✔ overhead transparency/ projector

Implementation

In this activity, children will have the opportunity to draft a rule that they believe should become a "law" in the classroom. Copy the Drafting a New Law reproducible for every two children, and make one copy on an overhead transparency. Use the transparency to model how to complete the reproducible. Divide the class into pairs, and give each pair a reproducible. Give children time to create a new classroom law and complete the form. Then, ask each pair to present their law and try to convince the other children why it would be beneficial and important. Invite the class to vote on each proposed law. If two-thirds of the class votes in favor of the new law, then it becomes one—majority rules. (However, there can be veto power from the teacher if it is a completely unreasonable law such as eating ice cream every day or never having homework.) Keep track of the new laws, since you will then need to discuss as a class the punishments they think are fair for the lawbreakers. Before the voting begins, teach the children some coping skills. Tell them that most ideas do not get passed as laws. Explain that sometimes the author of an idea needs to make many changes and explain it in different ways before it will be voted as a law. Sometimes, the author has to come up with a whole new idea. Introduce children to the democratic process in a fun, meaningful way by modeling
losing a vote. Tell them that you want to pass a law that children should have to go to school on weekends and never have recess. Have the class vote on it. When you lose say *Well, I guess I will just have to come up with a new idea! But, I won't give up!*

Integrating Our Country and World with Reading Instruction © 2002 Creative Teaching Press

Names _____   Date _____

Drafting a New Law

❶ What is your idea?

_____

❷ Why would it make our classroom a better place?

_____

❸ Who would be in charge of enforcing the law?

_____

❹ Why would this be a fair law for everyone?

_____

❺ What would be a fair punishment for breaking the law?

_____

Picture of someone following our law:

Class Vote Results:

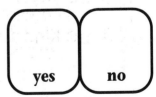

Did our idea become a law?

_____

Catch a Clue

What will we learn about in our reading today?

oceans

continents

states

maps

Our Clues

❶ We will be learning about things you can see on a map.

❷ People live on them.

❸ There are seven altogether on earth.

❹ They are large areas of land.

Concept Map

Facts we already know about the **continents,** and the new facts we have learned

Continents

Integrating Our Country and World with Reading Instruction © 2002 Creative Teaching Press

Word Warm-Up

 NORTH AMERICA  SOUTH AMERICA AUSTRALIA  AFRICA

Which words might you expect to find in a story about the **continents?**

oceans	koala	gorillas
cold	travel	airplane
town	country	rain forests
visit	penguin	animals

Integrating Our Country and World with Reading Instruction © 2002 Creative Teaching Press

Continents

Dear Grandma,

Mom told me that you just came back from Australia. Did you see any koala bears? I know that they are not really bears. They just look like bears. She said that you want to visit each continent this year. My teacher told me a continent is a big area of land that has oceans all around it. She said there are seven continents in our world. They are Australia, North America, South America, Europe, Antarctica, Asia, and Africa. She showed us a map. She showed us where we live. We live in New York City. That is in the state of New York. New York is in the country of the United States. We live on the continent of North America.

I want to go to the continent of South America. There are rain forests there. There are lots of animals. Some animals that live there are the tree frog, toucan, and zebra butterfly. Have you been there?

I know where you live. You live in the city of Venice. It is in the country of Italy. Do you know what continent you live on? I do. You live in Europe. We do not live on the same continent. Now I know that you will have to fly to my continent over the Atlantic Ocean to visit me.

Do you know how cold it is on the continent of Antarctica? It is ice cold! I do not think that you should go there. You are not a penguin! You might catch a cold.

My dad said he went to the continent of Asia when he was young. He saw the Great Wall of China. Have you seen it? I found out that the giant pandas come from Asia.

I think you should go to the continent of Africa. You can go to the jungle. It is warm there. You can see lions and elephants there. When you are done visiting the continents, will you come to North America to see me? I miss you so much!

Love,

Franco

Integrating Our Country and World with Reading Instruction © 2002 Creative Teaching Press

Comprehension Questions

? Literal Questions

❶ What are the seven continents?

❷ Where exactly does Franco live?

❸ What does Franco want his grandma to see in Africa?

❹ Why doesn't Franco want his grandma to visit Antarctica?

? Inferential Questions

❶ Describe the differences between a city, state, country, and continent.

❷ Why does Franco's grandma need to travel by plane to visit him?

❸ Which continents do you think his grandma still needs to visit for the first time?

❹ Why is it important for you to know about the different continents?

? Making Connections

❶ Where do you live? What is the name of your city, state, country, and continent?

❷ Which continents would you like to visit someday? Why?

❸ What animals live on each continent that you are interested in?

Integrating Our Country and World with Reading Instruction © 2002 Creative Teaching Press

Sharpen Your Skills

1 If you put these words in alphabetical order, which word would come last?

    ○ Antarctica   ○ Africa

    ○ Australia   ○ Asia

2 What two words make up the contraction "hasn't" in this sentence?

    Grandma **hasn't** been to the continent of Africa.

    ○ have not   ○ has not

    ○ had not   ○ here not

3 Which word or phrase best completes this sentence?

    Grandma _____ to Australia to see the koalas.

    ○ traveling   ○ was traveled

    ○ traveled   ○ travel

4 What punctuation mark should go at the end of this sentence:

    Would you most like to visit Australia or Asia

    ○ question mark (?)   ○ quotation marks (" ")

    ○ exclamation point (!) ○ period (.)

5 Which word would finish this analogy?

    Water is to **ocean** like _____ is to **continent**.

    ○ Asia   ○ boat

    ○ rivers   ○ land

Integrating Our Country and World with Reading Instruction © 2002 Creative Teaching Press

Name _____   Date _____

Marcus, Ben, and Patti are planning trips with their families. Each person will visit a different continent. Use the clues below to decide which continent each person plans to visit.

Clues

1 Ben will not see any rain forest animals. He will also not visit any jungles.

2 Patti will be traveling to the Amazon rain forest. She wants to see the toucans and the tree frogs. She lives in North America, so she will be traveling south.

3 Marcus will see some endangered animals. He will see lions roaming free in the jungle. He will travel east from his home in North America.

	Marcus	Ben	Patti
South America			
Africa			
Australia			

Marcus will travel to _____.

Ben will travel to _____.

Patti will travel to _____.

AFRICA

Pin the Continent on the World

Purpose

The purpose of this game is for children to practice locating the continents of the world.

MATERIALS

- ✔ Continent Pieces reproducibles (pages 51–52)
- ✔ construction paper or card stock
- ✔ crayons or markers (optional)
- ✔ scissors
- ✔ tape
- ✔ world map
- ✔ blindfold

Implementation

This game is a variation of Pin the Tail on the Donkey. Copy the continent pieces on construction paper or card stock. Color the pieces (if desired), laminate them, and cut them out. Put a rolled piece of tape on the back of each piece. Tape a poster-size map of the world on the wall at the children's eye level. Divide the class into seven groups. Put a blindfold on one child in a group, and give him or her one continent piece. Have the other children in the group use words (e.g., north, south, east, west or up, down, left, right) to guide the blindfolded child until he or she places the continent piece at its appropriate location on the world map. Have the other children in the class watch the other groups place their continent to reinforce their learning. Repeat these steps with each group using each of the seven continents. When each continent is placed on the map, decide with the class which continent is placed the most accurately. It is helpful to review the names and locations of each continent prior to the game. (Note: This activity can be done first without the blindfold to help children feel more comfortable with it. Then, repeat the activity using the blindfold.)

Integrating Our Country and World with Reading Instruction © 2002 Creative Teaching Press

Continent Pieces

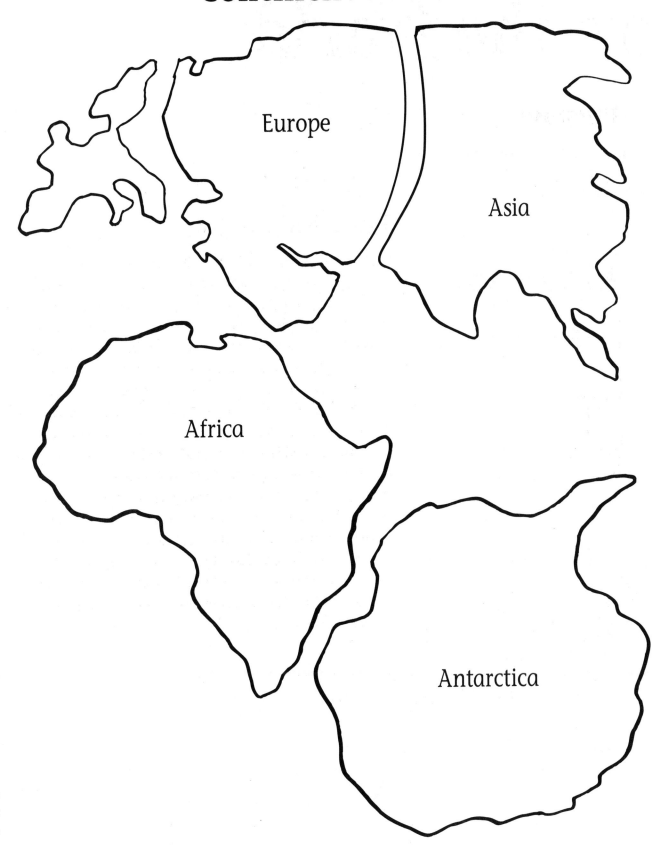

Europe

Asia

Africa

Antarctica

Continent Pieces

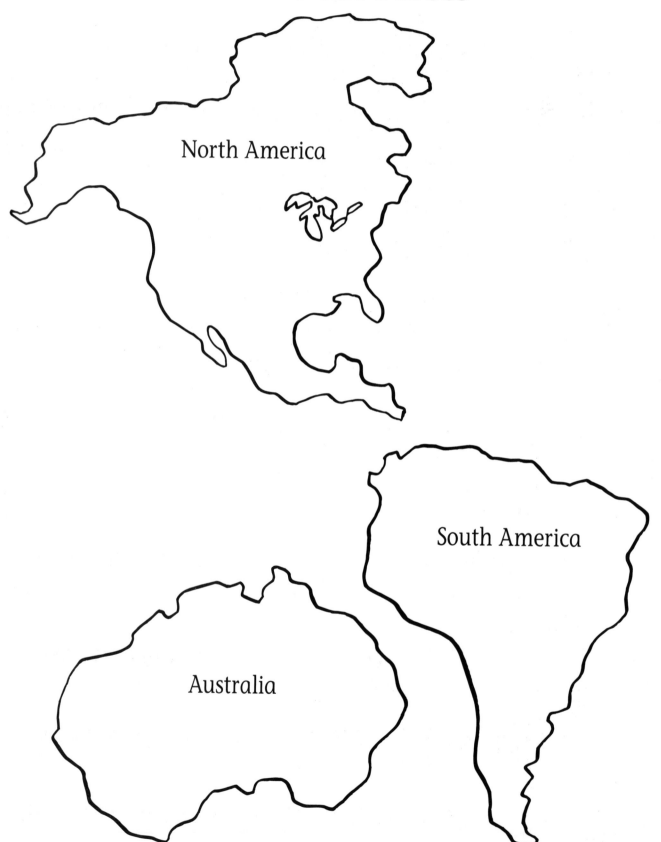

Integrating Our Country and World with Reading Instruction © 2002 Creative Teaching Press

Catch a Clue

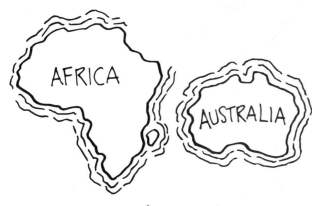

continents

bodies of water

vegetables

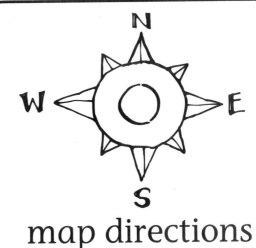

map directions

Our Clues

1 We will learn about things you can find on a map.

2 We will learn about things you can find on a globe.

3 We will not learn about pieces of land.

Integrating Our Country and World with Reading Instruction © 2002 Creative Teaching Press

Concept Map

Facts we already know about **bodies of water**, and the new facts we have learned

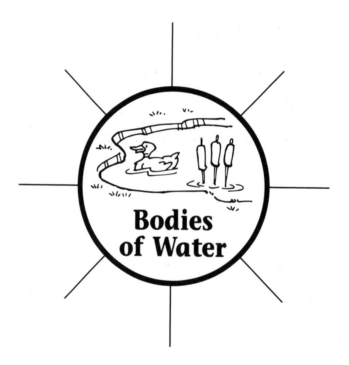

Bodies of Water

Integrating Our Country and World with Reading Instruction © 2002 Creative Teaching Press

Word Warm-Up

Which words might you expect to find in a story about bodies of water?

canoe	ski	climate
thirsty	rivers	horses
continents	flows	electricity
creatures	glacier	volcanoes

Bodies of Water

Did you know that our world has more water on it than land? It is true! Look at a globe. Each blue area is a body of water. Some are rivers, lakes, and oceans. The green areas show where there is land. You will see that there are more blue areas than green areas. How are they different? What do they look like on a map or globe?

A river is a large body of water that flows over the land in a long stream. It is made of fresh water. Most rivers start high on a mountain. A river ends where it flows into another body of water. This end is called the "mouth" of the river. It can flow into a bigger river, a lake, or an ocean. Fish and other small creatures live in rivers. There are rivers all over the world. Rivers will look like blue lines on a globe.

A lake is a large body of water that has land all around it. Lakes are formed in different ways. Some lakes were made from a

Integrating Our Country and World with Reading Instruction © 2002 Creative Teaching Press

glacier that cut a deep hole in the earth's land. Other lakes were made from past volcanoes. Some lakes were made when people blocked a stream to store up water. Rainwater fills up the hole and makes a lake. You can go on a boat ride, water-ski, or swim in some lakes. Fish live in lakes. A lake looks like an uneven-shaped oval on a map. Lakes can also be big or small.

An ocean is a huge part of our earth. In fact, if you split our earth into ten equal parts, seven of them would be oceans! The oceans are not filled with fresh water like rivers and lakes. They are filled with salt water. Many plants and animals live in the oceans. There are sharks, whales, dolphins, starfish, sea horses, and many other living things. There are four main oceans. They are the Pacific Ocean, the Atlantic Ocean, the Indian Ocean, and the Arctic Ocean.

All of these bodies of water are important for people and animals. Be sure to take good care of our rivers, lakes, and oceans. This way we can ski and swim in our water and have good water to drink!

Comprehension Questions

Literal Questions

❶ What is a river? What type of water is in a river?

❷ What is a lake? What can you do on a lake?

❸ What is an ocean? What are the four main oceans?

❹ How much of our earth is made up of oceans?

 Inferential Questions

❶ Compare and contrast rivers and oceans.

❷ Why do you think sharks do not live in rivers or lakes? Explain your answer.

❸ Why are oceans important to your life?

❹ What do you think happens when we pollute our earth's water?

 Making Connections

❶ Do you live close to any rivers, lakes, or oceans? Which ones?

❷ If you could travel to another continent, where would you want to go? How would you get there? Which ocean would you pass over?

❸ Do you like rivers, lakes, or oceans the best? Why?

Integrating Our Country and World with Reading Instruction © 2002 Creative Teaching Press

Sharpen Your Skills

1 If you put these words in alphabetical order, which word would come second?

○ ocean   ○ stream

○ river   ○ lake

2 Which word is a person, place, or thing (noun) in this sentence?

The oceans help us in many ways.

○ the   ○ oceans

○ many   ○ help

3 What punctuation mark should go at the end of this sentence:

I'm shocked to find out that seven out of ten parts of earth are water

○ question mark (?)   ○ exclamation point (!)

○ period (.)   ○ none of these choices

4 Which word is a descriptive word (adjective) in this sentence?

A river is a large body of water.

○ river   ○ large

○ is   ○ water

5 Which word would finish this analogy?

_____ is to **salt water** like **river** is to **fresh water**.

○ Lake   ○ Stream

○ River   ○ Ocean

Integrating Our Country and World with Reading Instruction © 2002 Creative Teaching Press

Name _____ Date _____

Dawn, Keisha, and Clayton each researched a different body of water. Use the clues below to decide which body of water each friend researched.

Clues

❶ Clayton chose this body of water because his favorite mammal is the dolphin.

❷ Dawn researched a body of water that contains many fish. She found a body of water that was almost as long as the state she lives in.

❸ Keisha researched a body of water that was created by rainwater collecting for years and years.

Lakes			
Oceans			
Rivers			
	Dawn	Keisha	Clayton

Dawn researched _____.

Keisha researched _____.

Clayton researched _____.

Integrating Our Country and World with Reading Instruction © 2002 Creative Teaching Press

Where in the Water World?

Purpose

The purpose of this game is for children to analyze and locate major bodies of water and continents on a world map in a fun, hands-on way.

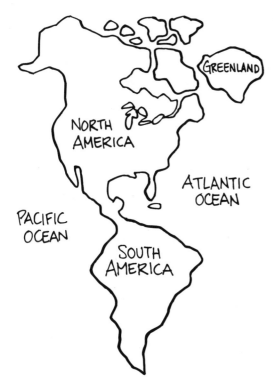

Implementation

Write several different sets of clues based on the World Map reproducible. Include clues related to measurement and geographical location. For example write *Start in the northwest corner of Africa. Then, move 1 inch south. Now, move 2 inches east. What body of water have you found?* Make a copy of the World Map reproducible for each child and an overhead transparency. Give each child a ruler and reproducible. Display the transparency, and guide children in labeling the oceans and the continents. Discuss the different directions (i.e., north, south, east, and west), and have children practice finding them. Also, model and have children practice using a ruler to find specific locations on the map based on inches (centimeters) from one place to another. For example say *Put your finger in the middle of South America. Use your ruler to go 2 1/2 inches northwest. What continent did you land on?* Tell children that you will give them one set of clues at a time. Ask them to use their finger and ruler to follow each step in the set of clues and then tell you what body of water or continent they landed on. When children give a correct answer, encourage them to model how they found it on the transparency. Ask children who also found the correct location to move their hands like a wave while making a swishing sound. To extend the activity, enlarge the world map to an 11" x 17" (28 cm x 43 cm) piece of paper. Give each child a copy, and follow the steps listed above. For more hands-on fun, pass out small fish crackers for children to use as markers for indicating the correct location. Invite children to enjoy eating the crackers at the end of the activity.

Integrating Our Country and World with Reading Instruction © 2002 Creative Teaching Press

World Map

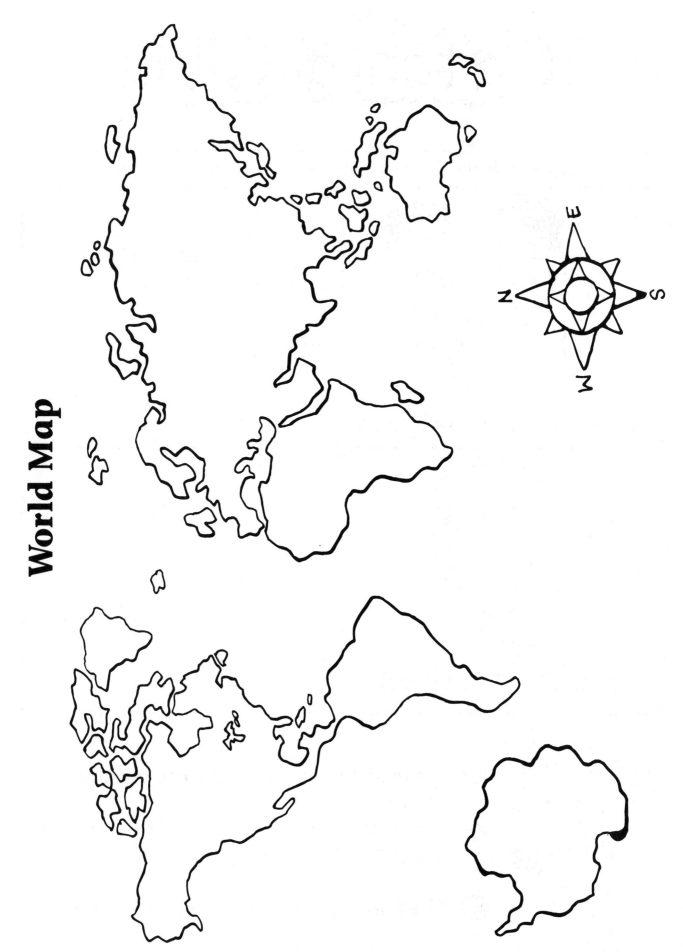

Catch a Clue

What will we learn about in our reading today?

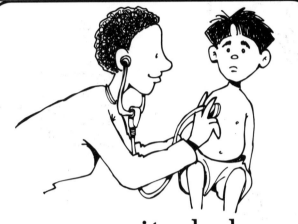

community helpers

teachers

famous Americans

ancestors

Our Clues

❶ We will be learning about people.

❷ Some traveled from countries far away to get to America.

❸ They are part of your family tree.

Integrating Our Country and World with Reading Instruction © 2002 Creative Teaching Press

Concept Map

Facts we already know about **ancestors,** and the new facts we have learned

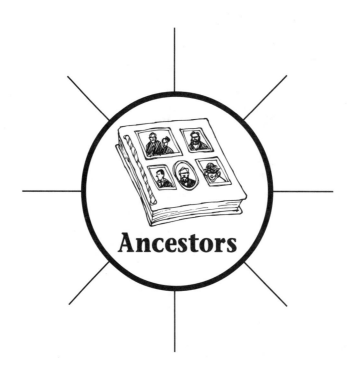

Ancestors

Integrating Our Country and World with Reading Instruction © 2002 Creative Teaching Press

Word Warm-Up

Which words might you expect to find in a story about **ancestors?**

king	war	relatives
careful	sailor	cousins
brave	community	doctors
pictures	generation	country

Ancestors

Today at school, we read a book about ancestors. As I walked home from school, I imagined my great-great-grandfather was a famous sailor. When I got home, I sat down for a snack. I asked my mom who my real ancestors were. She got out the family photo album.

First, she showed me pictures of my aunts and uncles. She said they were my dad's brothers and sisters. She was an only child, so I did not have any aunts or uncles from her side of the family. My mom thought it would be fun to make a family tree. My mom said it is a chart that shows each generation of a family.

We got a large piece of poster board. At the top, we wrote the names of my mom, dad, sister, and me. Then, we listed my grandparents' names. They are my mom and dad's parents. We listed all of their children, too. We continued to list aunts and uncles, cousins, grandparents, and great grandparents. We also wrote the country each person was born in.

Integrating Our Country and World with Reading Instruction © 2002 Creative Teaching Press

My mom told me a story as we made the poster. I found out that my great-great-grandfather, Sol, had to escape from the country he was born in. It was not a safe place to live anymore. There was a lot of fighting and war. One night, he was given a ride to a safe place. Then, he got on a boat to America. When he reached America, he had to go to Ellis Island. There were doctors there who gave him a checkup. This was to make sure he was healthy. If he wasn't, he might have had to go back to his country. My mom told me that Sol was my age when he came to America. "Was he scared?" I asked. "Yes. They had to leave so quickly, that he could not bring anything with him on the boat. Also, he did not speak English. This made it hard for him to talk to people and to read signs," my mom said.

I felt so lucky that I did not have to go through all of that! Although I am not related to a famous sailor, I learned that my ancestors are special. They helped make my life easier.

Comprehension Questions

? ### Literal Questions

1 What is a family tree?

2 What are ancestors?

3 Who did the boy in the story imagine his great-great-grandfather to be?

4 What did the boy in the story find out about his great-great-grandfather, Sol?

? ### Inferential Questions

1 Do you think the boy's mom thought their ancestors were important? Explain your answer.

2 Why did the boy in the story make a family tree with his mom?

3 Name three reasons why you think Sol was scared when he came to America.

4 Why do you think people left their countries to come to America?

 ### Making Connections

1 Did any of your ancestors come from another country? Which countries did they come from? Why did they come to America?

2 If you had to move to a new country without bringing anything at all, how would you feel? Explain your answer.

3 What could you do to make someone feel welcome into your country? Into your class?

Integrating Our Country and World with Reading Instruction © 2002 Creative Teaching Press

Sharpen Your Skills

1 If you put these words in alphabetical order, which word would come first?

    ○ ancestors   ○ family tree

    ○ Ellis Island   ○ countries

2 What two words make up the contraction "didn't" in this sentence?

At first, he **didn't** know what a family tree was.

    ○ do not   ○ does not

    ○ did not   ○ don not

3 Which word is an action word (verb) in this sentence?

The boy imagined that his great-great-grandfather was a sailor.

    ○ great   ○ imagined

    ○ boy   ○ sailor

4 What do the quotation marks (" ") in this sentence mean?

"Let's make a family tree," she said.

    ○ slow down   ○ read faster

    ○ she is excited   ○ someone is talking

5 Which word best completes this sentence?

They had to leave so _____, that he could not bring anything with him on the boat.

    ○ quicker   ○ quickest

    ○ quick   ○ quickly

Name _____   Date _____

Shana, Chou, and Miguel are learning about their ancestors. They are each imagining what they think their ancestors may have done long ago. Use the clues below to decide what each person is imagining.

Clues

1 Miguel thinks that maybe his ancestors created something important long ago.

2 Shana thinks that her great-great-grandfather lived with water all around him and was an important man.

3 Chou lives on a houseboat. He thinks that he knows why his parents like living on a houseboat.

	Shana	Chou	Miguel
Famous Inventor			
Captain of a Ship			
King of an Island			

Shana's ancestor was a _____.

Chou's ancestor was a _____.

Miguel's ancestor was a _____.

Integrating Our Country and World with Reading Instruction © 2002 Creative Teaching Press

Relative Research

Purpose

The purpose of this activity is for children to learn more about their family history, gain an understanding of various cultures, and see how other cultures are the same as and how they differ from America. Children will also practice their interviewing and presentation skills.

MATERIALS

✔ Relative Research reproducible (page 72)
✔ lined writing paper
✔ blank white paper

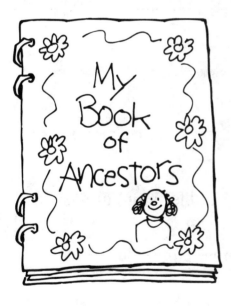

Implementation

Prior to this activity, send parents a note that explains the upcoming project. Tell parents that children will interview a family member to learn about his or her past. Encourage parents to brainstorm with their child which relative would be the most appropriate to interview. Have parents offer any needed assistance to their child with the interview (e.g., driving the child to see the relative, calling the relative on the phone, reading a question with difficult words, or spelling words correctly). Then, tell children that they will interview a relative as a way to learn more about history and ancestry. Give each child a Relative Research reproducible. Read aloud and discuss each question. Model with a child how to ask a question from the list. Then, have children practice asking one another questions from the list. Send home the research reproducible, and ask children to write their answers on it or on a separate sheet of paper. Allow children a week or two to complete the interview, and encourage them to bring in pictures that represent their research. Have children bring the completed reproducible back to class for an additional activity and oral presentation. Ask children to create an "ancestry book" in class. Have them write each piece of information on a separate piece of lined paper. Tell them to illustrate each page on blank paper. Invite children to color a cover for their book and place their pages in order. Staple each child's pages to his or her cover. Encourage children to share their ancestry book with the class.

Name _____ Date _____

Relative Research

Directions: Pick a relative that you would like to interview. Ask him or her each question below. Write each response next to the question or on a separate piece of paper.

Person you are researching: _____

1 Where were you born?

2 Where were your parents born?

3 Do any of your relatives still live in that country?

4 If not, why and how did they leave?

5 Do you or your parents speak a language other than English? If so, which language?

6 What was life like for you growing up?

7 What was life like for your parents growing up?

8 What was the most difficult time you had in your life? Your parents?

9 What was the best time you had in your life? Your parents?

10 Do you have any special family traditions? What are they?

11 If you could tell me one story from your life, what would it be?

Integrating Our Country and World with Reading Instruction © 2002 Creative Teaching Press